Teens.library

*Developing
Internet Services
for Young Adults*

LINDA W. BRAUN

American Library Association
Chicago and London
2002

Cover and text design by Dianne M. Rooney

Composition by ALA Editions in Bookman and Barmeno using QuarkXPress 4.1 for the PC

Printed on 60-pound white offset, a pH-neutral stock, and bound in 10-point cover stock by Batson Printing

The paper used in this publication meets the minimum requirements of American National Standard for Information Sciences—Permanence of Paper for Printed Library Materials, ANSI Z39.48-1992. ∞

ISBN: 0-8389-0824-1

Printed in the United States of America

06   05   04   03   02   5   4   3   2   1

CONTENTS

FIGURES

PREFACE

In June 2001 the Pew Internet and American Life Project published a report highlighting how and why teens use the Internet. The report, titled "Teenage Life Online: The Rise of the Instant-Message Generation and the Internet's Impact on Friendships and Family Relationships," found that much of the appeal of the Internet for teens centers around the communications functions the technology makes available.[1] Using e-mail, chat, and instant messaging are favorite pastimes of many of today's teens. However, not many libraries or library websites provide features that give teens the chance to use these functions as a part of their programs or services. Therefore, there is a gap between what teens find most appealing about the Internet and what libraries are providing to teens via their websites.

There is a host of possible reasons for this gap. Many librarians don't have the technical know-how necessary to implement some of the high-tech features teens find most appealing. Librarians struggle to find ways to integrate features like e-mail, chat, and instant messaging into their services in such a way that they complement and support the libraries' vision and mission. Some librarians don't understand what the appeal of the Internet is to teens and think that it would be better if they just stuck with a book.

Each of the above reasons for moving slowly into providing library programs and services to teens via the Internet has validity. However, we are at a point in time where it's not possible to take things slowly and to wait to learn how to use technology or to see how well others succeed. Teens are finding they can go other places than the library to get the information they need or to communicate with others online. If library websites for teens don't pay attention to the features of the Internet teens are most interested in using, one day there may be no reason for those websites at all.

That's where *Teens.library: Developing Internet Services for Young Adults* comes in. In this book is information about how the Internet meets teens' developmental needs. Any librarian who is wondering why teens gravitate to the Internet, if the Internet can have any sort of positive influence on a teen's life, or what websites are available that help teens grow up to be healthy adults will find answers to her questions here.

Also included is information on what teens look for in a website or Internet resource and how libraries are integrating some of these same components into their own sites. This information is provided to start the creative juices flowing to help librarians develop their own ideas for meeting teen recreational, educational, and developmental needs via the Internet. And, while the creative juices are flowing, it's important to figure out how to get teens involved in the website-development process. Tips on doing just that are also included in *Teens.library.*

For those librarians who don't have a clue about where to start in creating a library website for teens, the information on web design, working with designers and technical specialists, and technology needed in order to get a site up and running will certainly come in handy.

Throughout *Teens.library* are notes about websites of interest to librarians serving teens and resources that can be used in developing a library website. URLs are included throughout the text. Anyone interested in easy access to these materials can visit the Teens.library website at http://www.leonline.com/Teens.library. The website will be updated regularly to include links to library websites for teens that demonstrate uses of technology that support teen developmental needs, links to teen library websites in which teens have been actively involved in the development process, and tools and resources to use when developing a website for teens.

Now is your chance to start developing a library website, programs, and services for teens that go beyond the ordinary by creating content and resources that support teen needs and use Internet technologies effectively and successfully. By doing so you'll provide teens with resources that engage, entertain, and support their developmental needs.

NOTE

1. Amanda Lenhart, Lee Rainie, and Oliver Lewis, "Teenage Life Online: The Rise of the Instant-Message Generation and the Internet's Impact on Friendships and Family Relationships," Pew Internet and American Life Project (Washington, D.C., June 2001). Available at http://www.pewinternet.org/. Accessed 1 October 2001.

ACKNOWLEDGMENTS

Thanks to Renée Vaillancourt, who was the catalyst I needed to write a book on this topic, as well as Melissa Orth of the Curtis Memorial Library in Brunswick, Maine, who graciously consented to allow herself and the teens in her library to act as guinea pigs.

Thanks also to the following:

Tracey Firestone, who pointed me in the direction of Lisa Heggum

Joyce Valenza, for permission to use the Springfield High School Virtual Library screen shot

The Search Institute (Minneapolis, Minn.: Search Institute, 1997), www.search-institute.org, for granting permission to reproduce the Search Institute's Developmental Assets

America Online, Inc., for permission to use AIM screen shots © 2001

Bolt, for permission to use its screen shot;

Linda Waddle, Young Adult Library Services Association, for permission to use the Teen Hoopla Say What? screen shot;

Teen services librarian Lisa Heggum (for permission to use the Pickering Public Library screen shot); webmaster Kayhan Boncoglu; and the library's incredible Teen Advisory Group.

1

What's So Good about the Internet?

Why is it important to integrate Internet resources into library services for teens? Teens enjoy using the Web, e-mail, chat, and other Internet functions. At the same time, however, you may be concerned about all the time it takes to help teens find and use those resources effectively and successfully. Although very often it's easier to find what a teenager is looking for in a book, it is important to think carefully about what is happening in the life of an adolescent and how the Internet can actually help teens to grow up successfully.

DEVELOPMENTAL ASSETS

As young adult (YA) librarians consider the integration of the Internet into their programs and services, they should first think carefully about teen developmental needs—physical, emotional, and intellectual. This chapter looks at the Search Institute's Developmental Assets for Adolescents (figure 1-1) and uses examples of websites to demonstrate how the Web meets these assets.

Developmental Assets provide a framework for looking at the developmental needs of adolescents. "This framework identifies forty critical factors for young people's growth and development.

	Category	Asset Name and Definition
External Assets	**Support**	1. **Family Support**—Family life provides high levels of love and support. 2. **Positive Family Communication**—Young person and her or his parent(s) communicate positively. 3. **Other Adult Relationships**—Young person receives support from three or more nonparent adults. 4. **Caring Neighborhood**—Young person experiences caring neighbors. 5. **Caring School Climate**—School provides a caring, encouraging environment. 6. **Parent Involvement in Schooling**—Parent(s) are actively involved in helping young person succeed in school.
	Empowerment	7. **Community Values Youth**—Young person perceives that adults in the community value youth. 8. **Youth as Resources**—Young people are given useful roles in the community. 9. **Service to Others**—Young person serves in the community one hour or more per week. 10. **Safety**—Young person feels safe at home, school, and in the neighborhood.
	Boundaries and Expectations	11. **Family Boundaries**—Family has clear rules and consequences and monitors the young person's whereabouts. 12. **School Boundaries**—School provides clear rules and consequences. 13. **Neighborhood Boundaries**—Neighbors take responsibility for monitoring young people's behavior. 14. **Adult Role Models**—Parent(s) and other adults model positive, responsible behavior. 15. **Positive Peer Influence**—Young person's best friends model responsible behavior. 16. **High Expectations**—Both parent(s) and teachers encourage the young person to do well.
	Constructive Use of Time	17. **Creative Activities**—Young person spends three or more hours per week in lessons or practice in music, theater, or other arts. 18. **Youth Programs**—Young person spends three or more hours per week in sports, clubs, or organizations at school or in the community. 19. **Religious Community**—Young person spends one or more hours per week in activities in a religious institution. 20. **Time at Home**—Young person is out with friends "with nothing special to do" two or fewer nights per week.

FIGURE 1-1
Search Institute's Developmental Assets for Adolescents

Category	Asset Name and Definition

Internal Assets

Commitment to Learning	21. **Achievement Motivation**—Young person is motivated to do well in school.
	22. **School Engagement**—Young person is actively engaged in learning.
	23. **Homework**—Young person reports doing at least one hour of homework every school day.
	24. **Bonding to School**—Young person cares about her or his school.
	25. **Reading for Pleasure**—Young person reads for pleasure three or more hours per week.
Positive Values	26. **Caring**—Young person places high value on helping other people.
	27. **Equality and Social Justice**—Young person places high value on promoting equality and reducing hunger and poverty.
	28. **Integrity**—Young person acts on convictions and stands up for her or his beliefs.
	29. **Honesty**—Young person "tells the truth even when it is not easy."
	30. **Responsibility**—Young person accepts and takes personal responsibility.
	31. **Restraint**—Young person believes it is important not to be sexually active or to use alcohol or other drugs.
Social Competencies	32. **Planning and Decision Making**—Young person knows how to plan ahead and make choices.
	33. **Interpersonal Competence**—Young person has empathy, sensitivity, and friendship skills.
	34. **Cultural Competence**—Young person has knowledge of and comfort with people of different cultural/racial/ethnic backgrounds.
	35. **Resistance Skills**—Young person can resist negative peer pressure and dangerous situations.
	36. **Peaceful Conflict Resolution**—Young person seeks to resolve conflict nonviolently.
Positive Identity	37. **Personal Power**—Young person feels he or she has control over "things that happen to me."
	38. **Self-Esteem**—Young person reports having a high self-esteem.
	39. **Sense of Purpose**—Young person reports that "my life has a purpose."
	40. **Positive View of Personal Future**—Young person is optimistic about her or his personal future.

When drawn together, the assets offer a set of benchmarks for positive child and adolescent development. The assets clearly show important roles that families, schools, congregations, neighborhoods, youth organizations, and others in communities play in shaping young people's lives."[1]

Considering the assets can provide key information on the kinds of support teens need from their libraries. It's then possible to extrapolate how young adult librarians can use the Internet to support these assets. Use the examples of websites provided in this chapter as a way to start gathering ideas of what can be accomplished in both public and school libraries serving teens. Sites listed in the examples therefore are not only useful as possible links for a library's website, but they also act as models of the features and components librarians should consider adding to their own sites.

Support

> *Young people need to experience support, care, and love*
> *from their families, neighbors, and many others. They need*
> *organizations and institutions that provide positive, supportive*
> *environments.*[2]

The support category of the developmental assets refers to the family, community, and school support that adolescents receive. This means that teens need to have relationships with nonparent adults and parents involved in their schooling and have a sense that they are a part of the neighborhood in which they live.

It's not uncommon for schools to provide websites for their students. These often highlight what's going on in classrooms and in extracurricular activities. Common on these sites are links to teacher and administrator e-mail. This enables parents to e-mail a teacher or administrator about what's happening in the classroom or a specific concern they may have for their child. This is one way that parents can become involved in their children's schooling.

School libraries can also use their websites to promote parent involvement and demonstrate the kind of atmosphere that is promoted within the library. Consider these two school library websites and how they address this developmental asset category.

FAYETTE COUNTY PUBLIC SCHOOLS MEDIA SERVICES DEPARTMENT

http://www.fayette.k12.ky.us/instructtech/trt11/LibTechServ/Default.htm/

The media services department, in Lexington, Ky., developed a website that teaches information literacy skills, discusses the role of the library in the school, and the department's budget. By including this type of material on the website parents are informed about what's happening in the school library, the importance of the school library in a child's education, and the monetary commitment required to maintain and run a high-quality school library. This kind of information helps parents learn what their teenager's library experience is like while at the same time discovering the important role a school library plays in the teenager's education.

SPRINGFIELD TOWNSHIP HIGH SCHOOL VIRTUAL LIBRARY

http://mciunix.mciu.k12.pa.us/~spjvweb/

A school library website can also reflect the climate in which students work. The image on the main page of the Springfield Township High School library, in Erdenheim, Pa. (figure 1-2), presents the library as an inviting and friendly place. One can tell from this image that the librarian has a sense of humor and that she is thinking about what the site's audience, high school students, will find appealing and interesting. Many school library websites simply provide text links and static images that link to the resources on the site. These might be useful but are not particularly appealing to the teen audience, and they might send the message to teens, their parents, and the community that the library is not open to specific needs and interests of individual teens.

Empowerment

> *Young people need to be valued by their community and have opportunities to contribute to others. For this to occur, they must be safe and feel secure.*[3]

When looking at the category of empowerment, it's important to note that this relates to teen opportunities for meaningful participation in their community and opportunities for success. Consider

FIGURE 1-2
Springfield Township High School Virtual Library

how the Internet can provide adolescents with opportunities to participate in their communities. The following websites provide useful examples.

CONSUMER EDUCATION FOR TEENS

http://www.wa.gov/ago/youth/

High school students developed this site for the Washington State Attorney General's office. It's a site that provides information on consumer issues of importance to teens, including tattoos, car buying, car stereos, credit cards, and Internet scams. Each section of the site includes information teens need to know when considering purchasing a particular item or becoming a member of a particular service.

What sets this site apart from other consumer education sites for teenagers is that teens are responsible for everything on the site—from the content to the design. When considering the developmental assets category of empowerment, this site therefore demonstrates that the state of Washington trusts and values youth because the teenagers were given the opportunity to create the site for themselves. It also demonstrates that teenagers can play an important role in their community as information providers. There is no doubt that a site like this serves the community in which teens live.

DOSOMETHING

http://www.dosomething.org/

When a teenager visits DoSomething she can learn what to do about issues that are important in her everyday life, from teen pregnancy to the environment and from eating disorders to gun violence. This site provides tips on how to take action on each issue and also gives teens the chance to tell others what they think about the issue being addressed. DoSomething gives teens a place to turn when they aren't sure how to handle troubling long-term or short-term situations.

DoSomething is exactly the type of resource that helps teens feel empowered and able to make a meaningful contribution to society. By giving teenagers ideas for handling difficult situations, the site demonstrates that teenagers can play useful roles in their communities. Since DoSomething provides information on handling issues of violence, it also helps teens to find ways in which they can feel safe at home, in school, and in their neighborhood.

Boundaries and Expectations

Young people need to know what is expected of them and whether activities and behaviors are "in bounds" and "out of bounds."[4]

It often seems to adults that teens want to live in a world in which there are no rules. What is really the case, however, is that teens crave rules. Without them they are often at a loss as to how to behave. However, when a child reaches adolescence adults often give him more responsibility and loosen the rules so he can have more opportunities for making choices and decisions in his own life. What happens then is there is sometimes a direct conflict between what teens need developmentally and adult decisions about giving teens a higher level of responsibility. This is why this category of the developmental assets focuses on the importance of providing rules and limits to teenagers.

To find out how a website can provide this type of support visit the following sites.

RADIO DAYS: A WEBQUEST

http://www.branson.k12.mo.us/langarts/radio/radio.htm/

A webquest is an organized activity in which students are presented with information on what they need to do in order to accomplish a particular task. As a result, by their very nature, webquests are supportive of the developmental asset related to boundaries and expectations. The Radio Days webquest, and other webquests, not only give teenagers information on what they need to work on, but they also provide details on how the project will be graded, thereby clearly outlining the expectations for a particular project.

TEEN SAFETY ON THE INFORMATION HIGHWAY

http://www.missingkids.com/html/ncmec_default_teensafety.html/

This web page provides information on Internet risks, how to spot problems, and what to do if a difficult situation presents itself. These guidelines clearly outline for teenagers what behaviors are appropriate when using the Internet. As a result, teens have straightforward guidelines for how they should, and how they are expected to, behave online. To adults this information may seem like common sense; however, that's not necessarily the case for teens, and it is important to give adolescents the type of information that addresses boundaries and limits.

Constructive Use of Time

Young people need constructive, enriching opportunities for growth through creative activities, youth programs, congregational involvement, and quality time at home.[5]

This category refers to how adolescents spend their nonschool hours and looks at time spent in creative and religious activities, sports, and "hanging out." Internet resources that support this category of developmental assets include sites that provide teens with opportunities to post their creative works and resources that provide adolescents with information on religion. The following two sites are examples of this category.

BELIEFNET

http://129.33.230.60/

If a teen is looking for information on or opportunities to connect with others to discuss religion and religious issues, this is the place to go. Beliefnet acts as a clearinghouse of information on religions and is filled with resources teens can use as they work to gain a sense of their own spirituality and to understand the religious beliefs of others. One of the services of Beliefnet is a daily e-mail newsletter that contains either a Bible reading; a Torah reading; or Buddhist, Hindu, or Muslim words of wisdom. Subscribing to one or more of these messages gives teens the chance to consider, each day, an aspect of their own and others' religious or spiritual life. The tools on the site that provide teens with methods for connecting with others so they can converse about religious issues are important resources as well. Without these, a teenager might not have access to people who are available to answer her religious and spiritual questions. Ultimately all of the resources at Beliefnet support a teenager's need to be involved in religious or spiritual activity.

TEENINK

http://www.teenink.com/

Teens who are looking for opportunities for involvement in creative activities will find TeenInk a resource that's well worth the time. At the site teenagers submit their creative works—poetry, prose, nonfiction, art, and so on—or access the materials submitted by others. Along with the teen-created content the site includes writing tips—general strategies, along with how to write a review and how to develop interview questions—and information on how to select a college and on how to prepare for a final exam. TeenInk not only provides opportunities for teens to express themselves creatively but also offers information on how to be successful in that expression, TeenInk is a worthwhile resource for teens to know about in order to use their time constructively.

Commitment to Learning

Young people need to develop a lifelong commitment to education and learning.[6]

This category focuses on how teens relate to their educational environment and how successful they are in that environment. In many ways, the Internet resources that support this category are those with which librarians are most familiar—websites that support school curriculum and school websites in which teenagers have influence over the content and design. However, there are also resources that one might not at first consider when thinking about commitment to learning, yet they most certainly do support this teen need.

CHAPTER-A-DAY

http://www.chapteraday.com/

Included in the commitment-to-learning category is the asset, "Reading for Pleasure." The Chapter-a-Day service is one way to help adolescents learn about books they might want to read for fun. Teenagers who subscribe to the Chapter-a-Day service receive a daily e-mail, Monday through Friday, with a chapter from the book being promoted for that week. That means that every weekday teenagers are reminded via their e-mail about reading. It also means that once a teen starts reading a book through the Chapter-a-Day service, he might be more likely to want to finish that book and visit the library to get a copy. The teenager who subscribes to the service could possibly read at least one chapter of a book every day, thereby supporting that area of the developmental assets.

MAD SCI NETWORK

http://www.madsci.org/

There are many websites that help students with homework. Some sites provide links to resources that aid students working on specific subjects; others are filled with content on a particular topic. There are sites that give step-by-step directions on how to accomplish a particular task and also sites that allow teenagers to connect with experts in order to locate information that supports their homework need. Often this human connection helps engage a student in the topic and also motivates her to try to achieve a high level of homework success. Mad Sci Network is a resource that offers this valuable service.

At Mad Sci Network professional scientists answer questions submitted by students of all ages. When visiting the site students can search the database of questions and answers to see if someone else previously had the same question. They can even search by grade level to find out if someone their age asked the question and received a useful answer. If the question isn't available in the archives, teenagers can submit the question themselves. If the question is appropriate to the purpose of the site, a professional scientist will send an answer within two weeks—although the site does explain that a good number of questions are answered in a shorter period of time.

Why would teenagers be motivated to use a site like Mad Sci Network to support homework needs? Because they can find out what information other teenagers have been seeking and can communicate with a professional to find the answer. The interaction on the site is its best selling point for adolescents.

Positive Values

Youth need to develop strong values that guide their choices.[7]

Teenagers appreciate honesty in others. As a matter of fact, a poll performed by Teen Research Unlimited found that the most important thing advertisers should do when marketing to teens is to be honest.[8] Adolescents also look for opportunities to take part in projects that give them the chance to make a difference. When looking at what's available to teens, librarians should consider Internet resources that support these developmental assets.

SERVENET

http://www.servenet.org/

SERVEnet matches volunteers with organizations seeking assistance. All a teen needs to do when he visits the site is type in his

zip code. Once he does that he'll have access to a list of organizations he can contact in order to offer volunteer help. The listing
includes basic information about the sponsoring organization, age
levels of volunteers sought, and contact information. There are
also opportunities to volunteer virtually. For example, teens can
become SERVEnet Ambassadors. Ambassadors work in their
communities to help nonprofits realize the possibilities inherent in
using the Internet in volunteering and to make connections
between volunteers and local organizations.

SERVEnet enables teenagers to take personal responsibility,
demonstrate caring for others, and participate in meaningful
activities that might help them to make a difference in the world
in which they live.

KIDS CAN MAKE A DIFFERENCE

http://www.kids.maine.org/index.htm/

The whole point of this website is to give middle and high school–age
children opportunities to help end poverty and hunger. In an effort
to make that happen, the site includes a list of things kids can do
and overviews of what other kids around the country have already
achieved. Another method the site uses to get teenagers involved is
a bulletin board where teens post and respond to messages on the
topic. Through the resources it provides and the connections it
makes, this website goes a long way to helping teens understand
the importance of equality and social justice.

Social Competencies

> Young people need skills and competencies that equip them
> to make positive choices, to build relationships, and to succeed
> in life.[9]

Several of the assets associated with the social competencies category speak to a teenager's ability to behave appropriately in
social situations, to make good decisions regarding what they do
with their time, and to be able to handle peer pressure. When
Teen Research Unlimited asked teens what they hated the most
about being a teen, the answer was peer pressure.[10] Internet

resources that support the social competencies category might not come to mind quickly, but they do exist. The following provides two examples.

TEEN ADVICE ONLINE

http://www.teenadvice.org/

Teens who are looking for help and support as they work through issues in their lives will find Teen Advice Online to be a useful resource. Included on the site are articles written by teens on a wide array of topics. These include everything from sexuality to friendship and from drugs and alcohol to happiness. These articles provide teens with a great opportunity to read what their peers have to say and to use peer experience and insights in order to make their own decisions about how to behave in difficult situations.

Teen Advice Online also sponsors a question-and-answer service. Teens submit a question on a topic of concern and receive an answer from one of the teen counselors involved with the site. The question-and-answer service supports the social competency category in two different ways. By enabling teens to advise their peers, the site gives adolescents the chance to practice skills of empathy, sensitivity, and friendship while at the same time taking into consideration issues of culture, race, and background. Teens who receive answers from Teen Advice Online need to practice their own decision-making skills to determine if the advice provided is useful and appropriate to their particular need and situation.

TELL-US-YOUR-STORY.COM

http://www.tell-us-your-story.com/

Integral to the idea of interpersonal and cultural competence is that a teen needs to understand what it's like to live a certain way or be a part of a particular group—ethnic, cultural, racial, and so on. Tell-Us-Your-Story.com is a site for people with disabilities and those who live, work, or go to school with people with disabilities. On the site teens find stories of what life is like living with a disability. There are also discussion forums on topics including loneliness, self-respect, and embarrassing situations. Teens can submit their own stories about their relationships with people with disabilities or their own life as an adolescent with disabilities, or they can post a message to one of the discussion boards. First-hand accounts such as these provide teens with honest representations of what the lives of others, in this case people with disabilities, are like.

Positive Identity

Young people need a strong sense of their own power, purpose, worth, and promise.[11]

When considering the category of positive identity it is important to think about issues related to teen struggles with self-definition. Websites that support this category provide teens with a window into other people's lives, thereby providing adolescents with ideas about how they might want to conduct their own lives. These sites also show teens as successful members of society with options for a bright future.

U.S. NEWS AND WORLD REPORT: COLLEGE

http://www.usnews.com/usnews/edu/college/cohome.htm/

Many teens live for the day when they will finish high school. Sometimes they look forward to the next step in their life with trepidation and sometimes they anticipate college with great excitement. No matter how a teen feels about this stage in life, it's important that she knows she can determine what that next step will be and ensure that it will be a positive one.

The U.S. News and World Report website on college is one place where teens considering college can gain control over that decision. In many ways, this site is a one-stop shop for information about college, the college application process, and financial aid. Among the resources on the site is a comprehensive search tool that enables visitors to set specific criteria related to what they are looking for in a college, calculators for figuring out exactly what college will cost, and a class scheduler. Using the tools available, a teenager can make well-informed decisions about college attendance.

WHAT'S THE POINT?

Here are some points to consider when thinking about how the Internet supports teen developmental needs and the impact of that on library programs and services.

Access to Resources beyond Those Required for Educational Support

Teens need access to resources and tools that help them connect to the world in which they live. Young adult librarians should seek out websites and other Internet tools that provide teens with opportunities for participating in meaningful activities, discovering themselves, expressing themselves creatively, and learning how to behave appropriately in a variety of situations.

Chat, E-Mail, Discussion Boards, and Other Forms of Internet Communication

Consider how important it is for teens to discover methods for connecting positively with peers and adults. This helps them to determine their value systems, be socially competent, improve their self-image, and learn a new skill or topic. Librarians should seek out resources that help teens achieve these connections.

Teen Involvement in Development of Library Web Resources

Librarians serving young adults should actively seek out methods for teens to play a role in determining the design and content of the Internet resources provided by the library. Opportunities for empowerment, constructive use of time, and social competencies abound when teens are encouraged to join youth participatory activities. You can read more about teen involvement in website development in chapter 4.

Interactive Connections

Are there bulletin boards that promote discussion between teens and librarians (or other adults) around books, learning, and community on your website? If not, analyze how you might integrate interactive content on your website as a means of providing teens with the skills they need to become lifelong learners and successful adults.

SUMMING UP

When considering what Internet resources to make available to teens, think carefully about teen developmental needs and how to help meet those through technology. You can read more about how to accomplish that task in chapter 3.

Remember, teens need more from librarians than homework support. And of course it's also important to remember that the Internet is just one tool to use when assisting teenagers with their resource needs. Virtual and face-to-face interaction with librarians and other supportive adults is also key to their successful interaction with information in its assorted forms. By thinking carefully about what is happening in teen lives—emotionally, intellectually, and physically—you will be able to make good decisions about the role the Internet plays in their lives.

NOTES

1. Search Institute, Developmental Assets: An Overview. Available at http://www.search-institute.org/assets/. Accessed 28 July 2001.
2. Ibid.
3. Ibid.
4. Ibid.
5. Ibid.
6. Ibid.
7. Ibid.
8. Peter Zollo, *Wise Up to Teens: Insights into Marketing and Advertising to Teenagers* (Ithaca, N.Y.: New Strategist, 1999), 287.
9. Search Institute, Developmental Assets.
10. Zollo, *Wise Up to Teens,* 212.
11. Search Institute, Developmental Assets.

2

What Teens Want on the Internet

In June 2001 the Pew Internet and American Life Project published a report titled "Teenage Life Online: The Rise of the Instant-Message Generation and the Internet's Impact on Friendships and Family Relationships." As a part of their research the project sponsored online discussion groups with teens. The following is from one of those discussions:

> "The Net is an awesome thing," wrote a fifteen-year-old boy in the Greenfield Online discussion group. . . . "Who would have thought that within the twentieth century, a 'supertool' could be created, a tool that allows us to talk to people in other states without the long distance charges, a tool that allows us to purchase products without having to go to the store, a tool that gets information about almost any topic without having to go to the library. The Internet is an amazing invention, one that opens the door to mind-boggling possibilities. As a friend of mine would probably say, 'The Internet rules!!!!!!!'"[1]

In this quote it's possible to "hear" the excitement many teens feel about the Internet and to gain insight into the Internet features that most appeal to teenagers—communication, shopping, and information gathering. Missing from the list, but still of interest to teens, is using the Internet to play games and download

17

music. This chapter looks at some of these Internet activities and functions, why they are popular with teens, and what the implications of these are for library service to young adults.

COMMUNICATION

It's no secret to librarians that teens coming to the library like to use instant messaging (IM), chat, and e-mail. (Each of these technologies enables teenagers to communicate, in real time, with others around the world. See figure 2-1 for more information.) As a matter of fact, many librarians have said, "I often see two teens sitting next to each other at library computer workstations. Each

---

Chatting and instant messaging are common ways for people to spend their time. The question is, What are people doing when they spend time that way? To help answer that question, here's a brief overview of what chat and instant messaging are.

Chat

When people refer to chat, they are usually talking about joining a discussion, in real time, with other people on the Web. Usually to do this people go to chat "rooms" organized around a topic of interest. For example, someone might visit Yahoo! chat and go to a room devoted to wrestling. In that room she'll see the login names of the other people in the room and be able to take part in the conversation that's taking place. Any messages she types in at the chat room will display instantly on the monitors of all of the people in the chat room at that time. (It's also possible to take part in audio chat where what someone says into a microphone attached to the computer is heard by all the people—who have speakers or headphones—in the room.)

Instant Messaging

Instant messaging is a term used to refer to conversations people have, in real time, with a select group of people or a particular person. Instant messaging requires installation of software on the computer. Popular instant messaging software includes ICQ, AOL Instant Messenger, and Yahoo! Messenger. When the software is installed it can be set up to let the user know whenever her friends, family members, and so on are online and available to talk. The user sets up a "buddy list"—information about people with whom she wants to instant message. Then whenever someone on the buddy list is online the user is alerted and can communicate with that person at that time.

FIGURE 2-1
What are chat and instant messaging?

is using e-mail, IM, and chat. With whom are they communicating? Each other!" In other words, teens often use electronic communication tools to talk to each other even when they can just as easily have a face-to-face conversation. Many librarians wonder why that is.

Some light is shed on the topic in the *Rolling Stone* article, "The Secret Life of Boys." In this article the author, Jancee Dunn, begins by introducing readers to Joe, a fourteen-year-old in Edison, New Jersey. She writes:

> Hours can slip away as he Instant Messages friends on his list. "I'd say I'm online at least two hours a day probably," he says. "I guess that's a lot. But on the phone, you only have three-way. On AOL, you can talk to more people at once." He and his online community talk about the usual stuff: how school "sux," who likes who, the latest gossip.

> "He's on a lot," observes his mother, Donna, a pretty brunette. "At least four hours. He does it after school, then he eats dinner, then he gets back on, then I scream at him to go take a shower."[2]

The conversations Joe and his friends, or the two teens sitting next to each other in the library, are having seem, on the surface, no different than face-to-face or telephone conversations. The difference lies in the capabilities the technology provides. The Internet allows teens to expand their social circle and community beyond those who go to their school or live in their town and to engage in conversations that include a sometimes disparate group of people.

Another reason IM and chat appeal to teenagers is that these tools provide the chance to select whom they talk to by either ignoring messages sent by someone in a chat or IM session or by not including someone on their buddy list (a list of other users whom you want to know when you are online and available to talk). The Pew Internet and American Life Project discovered that teens are selective about whom they "allow" to join their IM conversations. Teenagers reported that they have different online personalities so that they can better manage their IM conversations. They make sure that only their best friends and close family members know the usernames they use in chat and IM sessions, which guarantees their anonymity (and safety) online.

What Does This Mean for Libraries?

The question that one might now ask is, "Why is it important to know about IM and chat when serving teens in the library?" As you read through the examples in this chapter of how teens use chat, consider these points:

- Knowing that teens look to IM and chat as a way to hang out with their friends and family, the library should consider how this supports the library's role of providing a place for teens to congregate in order to do homework or simply spend time with their peers.

- Since teens enjoy the possibilities IM and chat present for bringing friends and family together, the library should consider how they can use these technologies to bring teens from a variety of settings together to talk about books, reading, and so on.

- The library should consider marketing the availability of IM, chat, and other online communications tools as a way that teens can communicate with their peers both near and far.

- Since teens are sometimes selective about with whom they will communicate in IM or chat and sometimes take on "fake" personalities, librarians need to consider the impact on a library's IM or chat service. Does everyone in the chat room have to be identified as who they really are?

- Since most chat rooms require that one or more people in the room take the lead in order to keep chatters on topic, libraries should find ways to integrate chat as a means of helping teens learn leadership and facilitation skills.

- The wide selection of chat rooms and discussion forums provides a model of the variety of content that teens want to talk about. Libraries should consider how they could vary their website content and provide a resource that teens will want to return to over and over again.

Librarians may want to (or should) lurk in these chat rooms to find out what teens are talking about, what they are interested in, and to get ideas about how they can support teen needs and interests in the library.

Yahoo! Messenger, AOL Instant Messenger, ICQ

When using IM teens are likely to use AOL Instant Messenger (AIM), Yahoo! Messenger, ICQ (pronounced "I Seek You"), or an IM service provided by a specific website. Using each requires registering as a user of the IM system and may require downloading a piece of software. Once registered, a user receives the identification necessary (either a number or username) so others can add her to their buddy lists. When registration is complete she can also take part in conversations with other users, send e-mails, and send files and URLs to people with whom she is chatting.

Figure 2-2 shows the privacy settings and buddy list screens for AIM. Notice on the privacy settings screen that a user can specify if his information is available only to those on his buddy list and how much information about him is available to other "non-buddy list" users of the IM system.

Chat is different from IM in that chatters do not have the same level of immediate control over whom they chat with through their buddy list. However, many chat rooms allow visitors to send messages to specific individuals logged in at a chat room. It's also possible to set a specific individual's status to "ignore," thereby not having to read (or sometimes hear) a particular person's contributions to the chat session. As with IM most chat interfaces require the user to register to use the chat service. The username that is chosen in the registration process becomes the screen name used within the chat room.

YAHOO! AND EXCITE CHAT

http://chat.yahoo.com/

http::/www.excite.com/

Yahoo! and Excite offer teen-oriented chat as a part of their larger chat offerings. At each of these sites teens can find chat rooms on everything from dating and friendship to goth lifestyles and from chats specific to regions of the country to rooms devoted to a particular type of music or celebrity. (Sometimes these rooms are not within the teen-defined chat section and are instead within a chat area devoted to a type of music, and so on.)

If you visit one of the teen-oriented chat rooms (or any chat room, for that matter) you might notice that even though you are in a Backstreet Boys room or a World Wrestling Federation room the conversation isn't always, or even often, focused on the specific theme of the room. Teens might (and that's a big "might") enter a chat room with the idea that they'll talk about a topic of interest. However, what they simply want to do is to virtually talk and hang out with others with whom they have something in common—age, interests, locale, and so on. To stay on "task" someone in the chat room usually needs to take a leadership role. In that role she needs to facilitate the discussion, asking chatters specific

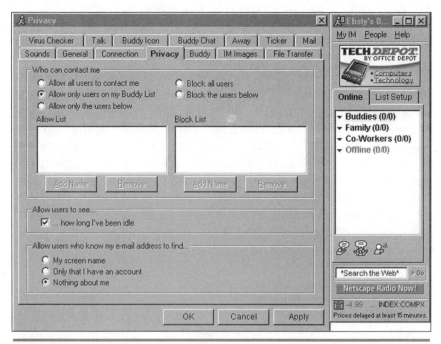

FIGURE 2-2
AIM preferences and buddy list screens

questions about the topic or throwing out ideas to get discussion going. This is no different than what is required for any kind of "good" conversation to take place. In virtual or "real" life someone needs to take the lead. However, if no one does take that lead, many teens are content to stick with a/s/l (see figure 2-3) and what some adults might consider conversations that lack focus.

KIWIBOX AND MADHIVE

http://www.kiwibox.com/

http://www.madhive.com/

Kiwibox and Madhive are two sites that cater to teens and sponsor topic-oriented chat rooms as well as chat events. Some of these sites also host chat events that push the capabilities of the technology. For example, for Valentine's Day Kiwibox (a site with a primarily female audience) and Madhive (a site with a primarily male audience) sponsored a Valentine's Day "dance." Teens who logged onto the chat on Valentine's evening selected a room based on their musical interest—alternative rock, hiphop, and so on. The appropriate music was streamed into each chat room and teens could "give cyber hugs, kisses—even buy [virtual] flowers for a date" while they chatted.[3]

So you visit a chat room and you realize you don't have a clue what the chatters are saying. First someone writes "a/s/l." Then someone writes "BTW." And all of a sudden you read ^5 on the screen. You are completely lost.

Don't worry, chat has a lingo all its own—it has to since part of the appeal of chat is its fast-moving conversation. If chatters had to spend time writing out full words and worrying about spelling all that appeal would be gone. All you need to do is bone up on some chat lingo and you'll be all set. A good place to start is Chatropolis at http://www.chatropolis.com/chat_dictionary.html/.

BTW (that's "by the way") a/s/l = age, sex, location and is used to find out the vital statistics of other chatters. ^5 = high five and you can probably figure out how that's used.

FIGURE 2-3
What are they saying?

BOLT

http://www.bolt.com/

Bolt is a website for teens that offers chat, but it also offers many other ways teens can communicate with each other. These include discussion forums, tagbooks (personalized discussion forums), e-cards, and notes. Each of these gives teens a chance to tell others what they think on a topic—from dating to art and writing and from health to college.

Teens visit Bolt by the thousands. The main page of the site includes information on how many Bolt members are currently signed onto the site. On one summer afternoon more than 7,000 members were logged in. What is it that brings all these teens to the Bolt site? It's certainly not the high-tech design. If you look at figure 2-4 you'll see that the look is straightforward and somewhat cramped. So the look isn't what draws teens in. Instead, it's the content: good information written for teens by teens and opportunities to communicate with peers about issues that are important.

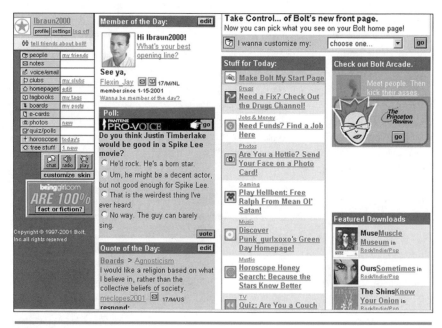

FIGURE 2-4
Main screen of the Bolt website

Creating Personal Chat Space

Most websites that currently provide chat also allow visitors to create their own chat space. For example, a teen might log onto Bolt and enter the chat area. Once there, instead of entering one of the predefined chat rooms he might decide to create his own chat space just for the group of people he wants to chat with at that time. All he has to do is decide on a name for the room and let the people he wants to join him in the room know it's available and what it's called. (Sometimes an official invitation is required to join the personal chat room, and sometimes all that's needed is the name of the room.) The personal chat space exists for the amount of time that chatters are in the room. In most cases, once everyone leaves the personal chat space the room no longer exists.

SHOPPING

Marketers and retailers are aware of the fact that many teens have large amounts of disposable income. (It's estimated that in 1999 teens spent $125 billion.) They also know that teens are using the Internet to find information in order to make smart purchasing decisions as well as to buy clothing, music, electronics, and so on. "Generation Y's power goes beyond their spending. Napster showed how young people who aren't tied to old business models and values can take control of what's marketed to them and exploit the Internet to change the rules of commerce."[4]

When selling to teenagers, marketers exploit technology as much as they can. This includes combining e-mail and web technologies to inform teens of good deals and limited-edition items. Here's an example:

> Using e-mail distribution service from @once, Giles [of Vans—a popular brand of teen shoes] sends his most loyal or promising customers messages offering limited-edition sneakers. . . . The shoe changes color when exposed to the sun's ultraviolet rays, something Giles thought could be demonstrated better online than in Vans' indoor retail stores. An e-mail included a 3-D, rotating picture of the sneaker changing color and a note promising that the first batch of shoes was being saved for online customers.

Vans.com saw a 20% click-through [the number of people who actually went to the site to look at the product via the link on the e-mail ad, which is extremely high for this medium as] promotion-rates of 2% to 5% are considered successful e-mail marketing. "We've created a very loyal consumer on Vans.com," Giles says. "We'll make a shoe that's available only online and only for a month so that the people who buy it have their own style of shoe."[5]

The click-through rate shows that teens responded well to this marketing technique. They liked getting a look at something that was being sold in a limited edition, and they also liked that they were specially targeted to receive the e-mail with the Vans information.

What Does This Mean for Libraries?

Knowing about teen shopping behaviors and how marketers are using technology to grab the teen consumer can give you some insight into how libraries can use the same techniques to promote their programs and services to the age group. Consider these as you read through the examples of teen online shopping behaviors:

Teens are interested in making sure they get a good deal. Libraries should use this interest to their advantage by providing teens with information that tells them about the deals libraries provide. This might include a tool by which teens could compare the price of purchasing a book at an online store versus checking it out of the library, or it could be that a library provides charts that show teens the "deal" they are getting by using library resources versus paying for them at stores or through database vendors.

Libraries should consider how they could use e-mail marketing techniques and special offers for "good" customers with the teen audience. Not only will this keep the library on the mind of the teens, but it will also help to ensure that teens become loyal customers.

As teens like going to websites that not only sell them something but also provide them with information and things to do, libraries should find ways to develop websites that provide teens with a place to hang out *online* along with a resource for finding information and tools to use in research.

YAHOO! SHOPPING, SHOPPER.COM, AND MYSIMON

http://shopping.yahoo.com/

http://www.shopper.com/

http://www.mysimon.com/

Teens use technology to hunt down the best deals. This means they might use sites like Shopper.com or MySimon to find out who offers the best price. It also means that they will look for companies to provide comparison charts that show why their product is better, or perhaps different, than that of the competitor.

The focus of Shopper.com is technology while the focus of Yahoo! Shopping and MySimon is broader and provides pricing information on a wide variety of topics—books, clothes, sports equipment, and so on. On each site all a teen needs to do is type in the name or type of product she is interested in purchasing, and a list of stores and prices for that product is generated. Then it's possible to compare item costs, shipping and handling costs, and delivery time in order to determine the best deal.

ALLOY.COM

http://www.alloy.com/

Many websites aimed at teens combine shopping with gossip, articles, chat, discussion forums, and so on. "Platform and other sites, like Alloy.com, iTurf.com, http://www.iturf.com/, and Hottopic. com, http://www.hottopic.com/, have risen to the top of online apparel sales partly because their sites attract young consumers by other means."[6] In other words, once a site brings teens in to read about celebrity gossip, life as a teen, and so on, they find reasons for looking at what's being sold in the site's online shopping area. Retailers are always looking for ways to keep the customer in the store as long as possible. On the Web, that's accomplished by providing more than a site that's only useful for making purchases.

While Alloy's front page includes a link to shopping in their main navigation bar at the top of the page, the information on shopping comes below the highlights of quizzes, surveys, and celebrity information. In other words, shopping isn't a hard sell at the site—at least not obviously—instead, the main promotion is for fun things teens can see, read, and do on the site.

The shopping section of the site is easy to use. Teens either look for items by a particular brand, category (shoes, glam, books, etc.), style ("Beach Babe," "Clean and Classic," etc.), or by SKU number or keyword. It's also possible to track the order once placed. The merchandise at Alloy certainly has the teen in mind with everything from bedroom lightbulbs to shirts, dresses, and jeans. Major brands are available, and if a teen isn't sure what to get there's a section with "Editor's Picks."

INFORMATION GATHERING

Often, I've heard librarians who work with teens say, "I don't know what to do, all the kids will use when they are searching is Yahoo! or Ask Jeeves. I can't seem to get them to use some of the other tools that are better for finding what they are looking for." That statement always reminds me of a line from an article written by Sara Weissman. In the article she wrote, "Search engines are pets. People just want to have one they can love."[7] For teenagers, Yahoo! and Ask Jeeves are pets that they are loyal to and that they think are loyal to them.

What Does This Mean for Libraries?

Information seeking is not solely associated with using search tools like Yahoo! and Ask Jeeves. It includes topic-specific sites and even the use of Internet communications tools. When libraries consider teen information-seeking behaviors and their impact on programs and services to young adults, they should consider:

> If search tools are a teen's pet, then librarians need to allow teens to keep their pet loyalty while at the same time finding ways to help teens find other pets to which they can be loyal. This means that a librarian shouldn't force a teen to use another search tool until he or she has seen that his or her own favorite can't do the job.

Librarians should remember that information can be gathered from a wide array of websites and that search tools are not the only means for finding out about where to find a particular piece of information. Teens respond to "specialty" sites that help them to navigate to the information they are seeking without too many clicks.

Library websites for teens should be intuitive in look and feel. Teens shouldn't have to hunt through several layers to find what they are looking for, nor should they have to try and figure out what the labels used for searching and links really mean.

As noted in the quote at the beginning of this chapter, teens are bypassing the library entirely to find information that meets their research needs. Librarians need to consider teen information-seeking behaviors and determine how they can meet the needs of those behaviors even if the teenager never comes into the library.

YAHOO! AND ASK JEEVES

http://www.yahoo.com/

http://www.aj.com/

What is it about Yahoo! and Ask Jeeves that creates loyalty among teenagers? It's the fact that both are seemingly easy to use. All a teen needs to do is type in the terms or question that needs to be answered and information of some kind appears. Even if the results aren't exactly what the teen is looking for, a teen has the feeling that she knows what to click on to try again or to find the information for which she is looking. For teens, it seems that using these tools does not require advanced or critical-thinking skills.

When teens visit the Web to look for information, they are looking for a tool that doesn't require that they learn a new skill in order to find the information. They are looking for information now, not after they learn how to search, so the tool has to be intuitive in how it is used. This doesn't mean that teens are not willing to learn how to use search tools, but when they are in the mode of finding information to meet their needs or a specific purpose, they want to go in and out quickly.

Consider the shopping sites mentioned above. At Shopper. com, a teen simply types in the name of the product he is planning on purchasing, and instantly he receives all the necessary information about the best price and the best deal. It doesn't require going through several levels in order to find the information needed. If the teen knows the name of the product, then in most cases only one or two clicks are required to find the information he is seeking.

It's important to remember that while teens do look for information electronically to support their homework needs, they also seek out information to meet recreational interests including music, movies, games, and hobbies. When teens look for this information they either go to trusted "pets" such as Yahoo! or Ask Jeeves, or they'll access tools specific to the content for which they are looking (Allgame.com for games, Ultimate Band List for music, or E! Online for Hollywood news and gossip). These, and other sites like them, are important sources of information for teens.

ALL GAME GUIDE, ULTIMATE BAND LIST, E! ONLINE

http://www.allgame.com/

http://www.ubl.com/

http://www.eonline.com/

These topic-specific sites are similar to the shopping sites discussed earlier in this chapter. When visiting any of these sites teens can either select links in order to browse through content on a particular topic, or they can type in a specific search to find information on the topic in which they are interested. The sites are straightforward in design and focus. The look is appropriate to the audience and purpose of the site. For example, E! Online uses celebrity photos to draw visitors in while All Game Guide has a somewhat dark and stark look that is reminiscent of the colors and design used in some online games. Each of these sites also has built a loyal following and is a trusted resource of topic-specific information for teens. They are some of the sites that could be classified as the Yahoo! and Ask Jeeves of their subject areas.

Each site's search tool gives a teen the opportunity to search within a particular field. At E! Online she can search by names, titles, new features, or products. At All Game Guide she can search by character, game, person, company, or platform. Ultimate Band List allows for searching by artists, songs, albums, and labels. These search tools enable teens to simply and easily hone in on the information that they are looking for. There's not a lot to figure out. And even if a teen doesn't select the appropriate field for his search, he is still likely to pull up information of value and not too much of it, so he will feel he's been successful in his quest.

SUMMING UP

Ultimately, the most popular sites and resources for teens combine the Internet features that are the most compelling. For example:

- Bolt mixes communications tools with information of interest to teens
- Alloy integrates chat with shopping and celebrity news and gossip
- Yahoo! provides chat, comparison shopping, search tools, and so on.

As librarics consider what they need to do to provide Internet-based services to teens, finding ways to integrate these different tools is an important first step in creating high-quality programs and services.

NOTES

1. Amanda Lenhart, Lee Rainie, and Oliver Lewis, "Teenage Life Online: The Rise of the Instant-Message Generation and the Internet's Impact on Friendships and Family Relationships," Pew Internet and American Life Project (Washington, D.C., June 2001). Available at http://www.pewinternet.org/. Accessed 1 October 2001.
2. Jancee Dunn, "The Secret Life of Boys," *Rolling Stone* (July 5, 2001): 102–110.
3. Shelly Emling, "Virtual Dance: Teens Can Point, (Maybe) Click," *Atlanta Constitution* (February 5, 2001): sec. D, 1.
4. Eileen Colkin, "Kids These Days," *Information Week* (February 12, 2001).
5. Ibid.
6. Nina Siegal, "Sell the Scene Not Just the Shirt," *New York Times* (June 7, 2001): sec. H, 40.
7. Sara Weissman, "Shoptalk: Teach 'Em What They Need," *netConnect* (spring 2000): 36.

3

Creating a Library Website for Teens

Chapter 1 looked at how the Internet meets a variety of teen developmental needs, and chapter 2 focused on what makes certain sites and technologies popular with teens. The focus of chapter 3 is on what libraries can do to provide high-quality services to teens via the Internet. This chapter considers information from previous chapters when presenting options and opportunities for librarians. It looks at what libraries are already doing, how services might be extended via the Internet, and covers briefly the technologies required to create the services discussed. (More information on technology requirements is available in chapter 4.)

WHAT'S UP WITH LIBRARY SITES FOR TEENS?

The best way to see what's happening on the Internet for teens in libraries around the country is through a tour of sites to see exactly how they are enhancing provision of traditional library services via the Internet. At this time, few library sites are taking full advantage of the high-tech Internet features that many commercial sites are using. As a matter of fact, most sites use their online space primarily as a way to link teens to resources they might use for homework or entertainment. The sites that go a little further employ methods so teens can:

- submit art, writing, and so on;
- communicate in real time with a tutor or librarian about homework needs; and
- obtain readers' advisory service in order to find books that meet their interests.

REFERENCE AND HOMEWORK SUPPORT

Links are the most common form of reference and homework support for teens on the Internet. A majority of library websites that serve teen users make links the primary focus of their sites. Of course, since it is important to provide teens with a collection of print and electronic resources they can use in support of their schooling needs, this is a key aspect of serving the population. However, links are just one way to help teens with their homework. Following are a few examples of other ways these needs are met via library websites.

CURTIS MEMORIAL LIBRARY, BRUNSWICK, MAINE, TEEN ZONE, BOOK A LIBRARIAN

http://www.curtislibrary.com/teenzone/booklibrarian.html/

Curtis Memorial Library's Book a Librarian feature is an interesting addition to their site for teens that includes links, information about the library, and a place to post writing or art. When a teen accesses the Book a Librarian page she can fill out and submit a form. This is the first step to making an appointment with the young adult librarian to talk about homework or research needs. On the form the teen is asked for her name and e-mail address and for information about her homework need. After receiving the form the young adult librarian contacts the teen to set up a time when the two can meet to look at different resources and discuss research strategies for finding the information needed. The Book a Librarian feature of Teen Zone is a definite match to the support asset as described in chapter 1.

BOSTON PUBLIC LIBRARY, BOSTON, MASS., ONLINE TUTORING

http://www.tutor.com/bpl/Default.asp/

In January 2000 the Boston Public Library launched a program that matched middle school students with tutors. Students who registered for the program visited their branch library weekly to meet with their tutor. However, except at the beginning and the end of the project, the students and tutors didn't meet face-to-face. Instead they met via the Internet, and the students used the library's computers for these meetings. The web-based interface used by students and tutors provided real-time chat opportunities, white board space in order to go over specific ideas and concepts, and the ability to exchange documents.

The website for Boston's online tutoring program includes the following statistics as a measure of the program's success during its first year:

- 80 percent report better grades in math as a result of tutoring
- 83 percent were more confident in math after tutoring
- 76 percent student attendance rate[1]

Online tutoring is an interesting way to use web-based technologies to support a teenager's commitment to learning. The integration of real-time technologies—chat, white boards, and so on—helps grab a teenager's interest. In other words, a project such as online tutoring meets teen developmental needs using technologies in which the group is interested.

CLEVELAND PUBLIC LIBRARY, CLEVELAND, OHIO, HOMEWORK NOW

http://www.homeworknow.net/

Of course, teens don't have homework questions only during the hours the library is open. And not all teens can get to the library when it is open to meet their schoolwork needs. That's where a service like Homework Now comes in. Homework Now uses the 24/7 chat-reference interface to help students locate and access materials they can use for their homework.

In order to access the Homework Now service a student enters his zip code. After authentication (the service is only available to students who live or go to school in the Clevenet Library Consortium area) the student selects the topic area in which he needs help (e.g., English, math, science, etc.). Following that selection the student is brought to a screen where he can enter his name, e-mail, and the question on which he needs help finding resources to use.

The interface of Homework Now divides the screen into two parts, allowing the chat conversation to take place on the right side of the screen while on the left the librarian helping the student can send information virtually, including websites, library catalog records, and so on. In this way the student and librarian browse through the resources together until each is satisfied the homework need is met.

By providing an e-mail address the student involved in the chat receives an e-mail transcript of the reference session. That means he doesn't need to write anything down. It also means that any information the librarian provides, for example, tips and tricks on how to find resources effectively, will be included in the e-mailed transcript. Students who receive reference assistance in this fashion not only have help finding the materials they need, but they also often receive information-literacy lessons, even though it's not something they are aware of at the time.

PROGRAMMING

Programming for young adults takes on a wide variety of forms in the traditional library world. Libraries sponsor workshops, book-discussion groups, teen-advisory programs, intergenerational programs, speakers, and so on. These programming efforts often give teens a chance to participate in the planning and organization of the event.

Programming on a library's website gives teens a chance to participate via a variety of online forms and forums. Teens might or might not be involved in the actual planning of the web-based program, but the online activities integrated into the site give teens the opportunity to participate in library events in a variety of meaningful ways. (See chapter 4 on how to get teens involved in the website development process.)

Following are a few examples of the ways libraries have brought teen programming to the Internet.

NEW YORK PUBLIC LIBRARY, NEW YORK, N.Y., TEENLINK, WORDSMITHS

http://www2.nypl.org/home/branch/teen/WordSmiths-Current.cfm/

WordSmiths is the section of New York Public Library's TeenLink site where teens submit or read poems and short stories by their peers. At WordSmiths there are poems about a variety of teen issues, from love to baseball and from the meaning of life to what it's like to grow up in a city. Teens from around the world are encouraged to submit writing to WordSmiths via the online form on the site. (There's also information on how to submit writing via e-mail or postal mail.)

The details of submission are defined this way on the site:

> To submit poems or short stories, you must be 12 to 18 years old. You may submit up to 3 poems and 1 short story a month or any combination of your work that does not exceed the equivalent of 4 typed, double-spaced, 8½" × 11" pages. Your submissions must include your name and age and a way to reach you. You may also add where you live and where you go to school. We regret that we cannot [accept] pieces submitted as class assignments at this time. Submissions from individuals are always welcome.[2]

TEEN HOOPLA SAY WHAT?

http://www.ala.org/teenhoopla/saywhat/index2.html/

When the Young Adult Library Services Association (YALSA) of the American Library Association (ALA) launched Teen Hoopla in 1997, the committee in charge of the website wanted to include something that would give teens the chance to talk with each other about topics of interest. The Say What? section of the site provides that opportunity. Every few months Teen Hoopla posts a new topic so teens can let their peers around the world know what they think. Past topics range from filtering and libraries to summer reading and from teen driving to dress codes. Figure 3-1 shows the main page of Teen Hoopla's Say What? section.

FIGURE 3-1
Main page of Teen Hoopla's Say What? section

Each Say What? discussion includes information on the discussion topic along with links to resources teens can check out in order to become better informed. Looking through the postings at Say What? it's possible to see that teens from around the world comment on the topics and have no qualms about having their opinions "heard." Looking at the discussion on body image one reads what teens have to say about their height and weight, the impact the opposite sex has on body image, how they feel wearing bathing suits in public, and the influence print and electronic media have on how teens feel about themselves. Many of the postings are signed with nicknames, allowing those who submit to the discussion board the opportunity to say what they think with relative anonymity.

The power of WordSmiths and Say What? in teen lives was visible following the terrorist attacks on September 11, 2001. Not long after these events WordSmiths and Say What? published content that gave teens the opportunity to communicate with others about their feelings. WordSmiths published a special edition devoted to work teenagers wrote as a result of the attacks. Say What? developed a discussion forum on the topic where teens could tell others what they were feeling. The ability to instantaneously develop a program to support teens in times of need is one of the highlights of the programming opportunities available through the use of Internet technologies.

WordSmiths and Say What? help teens meet several developmental assets including empowerment, positive values, and social competencies. Neither programming opportunity allows teens to communicate in real time with their peers, yet both are popular with teens. The presentation of the resources along with the opportunity to communicate with the world through creative and expository writing is certainly the reason for this popularity.

READERS' ADVISORY

The simplest and most common form of teen readers' advisory services on the Internet is the posting of web-based versions of booklists previously only made available in print. The following is an example of another way a library is using the Internet to provide readers' advisory services to teens.

SPRINGFIELD-GREENE COUNTY LIBRARY DISTRICT, SPRINGFIELD, MO., TEEN THING, INTERACT

http://thelibrary.springfield.missouri.org/teens/interact/interact.htm/

InterAct, a feature of the Springfield-Greene County Library District Teen Thing website, provides teens with opportunities to discuss topics of interest. Included in the InterAct section is an online book discussion group. As with the Bolt bulletin boards described in chapter 2, InterAct uses a threaded discussion forum format. That means teens post messages about the book under discussion and respond to what others have written about the book all within one web page. Posters, readers, and respondents can look through all the messages submitted in order to understand the discussion thread and reply appropriately.

When looking at the InterAct book discussion one might wonder why it doesn't have the same level of activity as the discussions sponsored at a site like Bolt. There could be several reasons for this. When developing this type of feature it's important for librarians serving teens to consider the causes of limited participation. Questions one might ask when thinking about this include:

Has the library marketed the resource to teens?

If marketed to the target audience, what marketing techniques were employed?

Are the books under discussion those that teens would be interested in reading?

What technology must a teen have access to in order to successfully take part?

How easy is it to find the discussion board on the library website?

What methods are being used to facilitate the discussion?

Is there something about the resource that will draw teen readers in over and over again?

Each of these questions needs to be considered before this type of feature is included on a library website. In other words, building it doesn't mean teens will come. Consider the Bolt website one more time. It's the array of discussion topics along with the large number of participants involved that draw teens to Bolt and keeps them coming back. Teens who post on Bolt want to know if someone replied to their posting. If responses are none or limited a teen might not come back, but if there's a real discussion going on then she'll return over and over to join the discussion.

Libraries just starting this type of programming need to consider how to keep things moving in the beginning stages of the service. The librarian might need to spend some time facilitating discussion online, responding to messages posted, asking questions of those taking part, and getting others involved in the discussion. In many ways, it's no different than leading a face-to-face discussion group. In both instances the librarian needs to be prepared and able to keep the conversation going.

If beginning an online discussion group, consider these tips for successful participation:

Ask teens to select the topics and materials up for discussion.

Advertise to make sure there's a ready, willing, and able audience.

Start the discussion with a question or comment that will pique teen participants' interest. For example, starting with a question like, "Did you like or dislike this book" won't get much response. However, asking a question like, "As you were reading the book what were the times when you stopped and said to yourself, 'Wow'?" is much more interesting to consider. Another possible question to begin with is, "What event or scene from the book did you find the most exciting, interesting, boring, and so on, and why?"

Be ready to respond to postings even if no one else is. Before joining in the discussion some teens will wait to see how the conversation is going. The only way to keep the conversation going therefore might be for you to respond to each posting.

Don't be disappointed if the thoughts of the teens posting on the discussion board aren't what was expected. For each posting, at least in the beginning, find a kernel of thought that might be of interest to other teens and facilitate a discussion related to that thought.

Try to ask more questions when responding to a posting instead of giving all the answers. That sets up an atmosphere of facilitated discussion and not a place for one person to lecture on what they think the book means, is about, and so on.

Don't worry about grammar, spelling, punctuation, and so on, in teen postings to the discussion board. Teens should feel like this is a space where they can write what they are thinking without having to worry too much about whether or not their sentences are complete or commas and periods are in the correct place.

Of course, a library has to start somewhere, so when developing an online book discussion (or other type of discussion group for teens) consider the tips above and draw from the example of Bolt. Diversify the discussion as much as possible, be ready to spend time in order to make it work, and market to regular teen library users and nonusers who might never have set foot in the door of the library—and certainly not in the library's young adult area.

WHAT IT TAKES

The library websites and possibilities described above use a variety of technologies. New York Public Library, Curtis Memorial Library, and Teen Hoopla's Say What? all incorporate online forms—two use a programming script, and one uses very basic HTML tags. The discussion board at Springfield-Greene County Library District integrates a threaded discussion forum that uses a script in order to function. Boston Public Library's Online Tutoring uses the software and hosting services of a company, Tutor.com, in order to implement the technology required for the interface. The homework help provided by Cleveland Public Library uses software configured appropriately for the needs of the library system.

In order to integrate those features into a library's website it's important to consider the different options available. Often there's more than one option for each type of interactive service. It's also important to think about who will be working on the site and the expertise each person involved in the development brings to the project. (More information about the technology required to implement interactive features on the library's website is included in chapter 4 and on the Teens.library website.)

Online Forms

The knowledge of the people working on the library's website will have an impact on the level of technology used on the site. The forms used at New York Public Library, Teen Hoopla, and Curtis Memorial Library provide a good overview of the different options available for feedback and other types of online forms. The most complicated of the three is at New York Public Library with the simplest form on the Curtis Memorial Library website.

At Curtis Memorial Library's TeenZone, instead of using a script that informs the server how to process the information submitted, the code that implements the form uses simple HTML tags to send the submission to a particular recipient's e-mail address. This type of form works well if there isn't a need to organize the gathered information into specific database fields or if it's unnecessary to provide the visitor with any specific feedback after they submit the form.

Teen Hoopla's Say What? feature uses a simple script that is implemented when a visitor submits his information. While, as with TeenZone, the information from this form is e-mailed to an address listed within the form tags in the HTML code, other aspects of the form are more advanced than the code used by Curtis Memorial Library. When a teen submits his thoughts to Say What? a new page is generated that thanks him for the submission and provides a link back to Teen Hoopla. Also, the script that is used for the form includes information about fields that are required for each submission. That means if the teenager doesn't fill in a required piece of information he is instructed to go back to the form page and add the missing component.

At the New York Public Library the WordSmiths form is the most complicated of the bunch. That's because the site uses a web-building application called Cold Fusion. Cold Fusion allows web developers to create highly interactive web content that can be manipulated and updated in a variety of ways. While the code used to create the form for WordSmiths is not any more complicated than that for the other two sites discussed, the interaction between the code and the Cold Fusion software and server allows for much more flexibility in the way the form is received and how the information is processed and organized once submitted.

Discussion Boards

As with the implementation of forms on a website, there are different options for the way discussion boards may be implemented. The simplest and most inexpensive option is to use a service on the Internet that provides the space and the technology needed to create and offer discussion forums. The amount of customization allowed with this type of service varies as does the quality of the technology and the support available for running the discussion. Page advertisements are the norm with free discussion-forum providers so if there are concerns about advertising on the website this is something to consider.

Portal sites also provide free discussion-forum services. For example, it's possible to gain access to a discussion board by starting a Yahoo! club. In order to enter the club and use the forum, teens need to log in with a username and password. That means that everyone participating in the discussion forum at the club has to register with Yahoo! in order to participate.

Another aspect to consider if using a portal service is that the URL that people see and use to access the forum is not the same as that of the library's website or domain name. For example, all URLs for Yahoo! clubs start this way: http: //clubs.yahoo.com/clubs/. Similarly, the look and feel of the forum will not match the look and feel of the other parts of the library's website for teens.

If the library has access to people who know how to configure discussion forums, then it's possible to create something that keeps teens at the library's website—the URL—and incorporates the look and feel developed for the site. (It also means more control over how the discussion forum works.)

Third-Party Applications and Providers

Both Boston Public Library's online tutoring project and Cleveland Public Library's Homework Now service use software applications developed by a third party. The interface currently used by Boston Public Library, in which students and tutors work together, is provided by Tutor.com, a company that specializes in live homework-help technologies.

For its Homework Now service the Cleveland Public Library uses a product developed as a part of the 24/7 Reference project sponsored by the Metropolitan Cooperative Library System in southern California. The product provides librarians with the software required to provide real-time reference assistance to patrons and is customizable to meet the look and feel of a particular library's website and the needs of a particular patron group.

The technology required to implement interactive services such as those at Boston Public Library and the Cleveland Public

Library require a high level of technical sophistication. For that reason they are best implemented using third-party products from companies such as Tutor.com and 24/7 Reference. The librarian can then spend her time considering how to promote and integrate the service so that it meets the needs of teens within the community.

WHAT ELSE IS POSSIBLE?

When deciding what types of Internet-based services to provide to teens it's important to begin by focusing on:

The library's vision, mission, and goals. These need to be discussed to make sure they are met effectively.

The uniqueness of the library's teen population. Consider this to make sure that the specific needs of the teens in the community are met.

The service responses developed by the Public Library Association (PLA) and published in *The New Planning for Results* materials prove useful when considering how to use a library's website in support of teens' informational and recreational needs.[3] Following are some examples of how the Internet might be integrated into the way a library meets specific service responses.

Commons

When focusing on teens, this service response relates to helping teens within the community meet each other so they can discuss topics and issues related to life within the community. If this service response is selected by librarians serving teens, a website might include:

Regularly scheduled moderated chat sessions where teens join with their peers to discuss topics of interest including school, sports, music, art, and so on.

Audio or video presentations by speakers and presenters who are of interest to teens. This might include live webcasts with community members with whom teens might like to chat.

Community members might include government officials, employees at local stores or other businesses, and so on.

Current Topics and Titles

In the young adult services context this service response focuses on helping teens locate and access information on popular culture and fulfilling teen recreational reading needs. If this service response is selected by librarians working with teens, a website might include:

A web-based readers' advisory tool. To find titles of interest teens type in the name of a book, genre, author, and so on, that they enjoy reading. The list of materials generated would be linked to the library catalog and a local or online bookstore so the teen could determine if an item was available in the library or for purchase.

Real-time chat sessions in which teens communicate with favorite authors. The transcripts of these sessions would be archived so teens who were not able to participate would still be able to read what authors had to say.

Formal Learning Support

When looking at library services to teens, this service response focuses on how libraries support homework needs. If this service response is selected by librarians serving teens, a website might include:

Personalization services. A teen sets up a website account by creating a user profile. The profile might include information on the books she likes to read, the classes in which she's enrolled, and so on. Then whenever she logs onto the library's website using her profile username and password she sees a list of resources that meet her interests and needs, including books, websites, and other materials that support the courses she is currently taking.

Pathfinders related to specific homework assignments. These pathfinders would include print and electronic resources as well as links to the library catalog and links to database subject headings related to the topic of study.

IS IT WORTH IT?

Of course, it's important to consider if developing Internet-based library programs and services for teens is worth the trouble. Boston Public Library's online tutoring project showed that by providing the service, middle schoolers increased their school performance. That certainly points to the value of providing web-based homework assistance and tutoring. But what about the effectiveness of programming and readers' advisory services via the Internet? Are they worth the time and effort? To decide, it's a good idea to think about the developmental assets presented in chapter 1, the information on teen use of the Internet provided in chapter 2, and the models of library Internet services covered in this chapter. By doing that it's possible to come to some conclusions:

- Providing library services for teens via the Internet meets a variety of developmental assets including support, empowerment, positive values, and social competencies.

- Library programs and services via the Internet make use of technologies that teens find appealing and want to be a part of.

- Internet-based library programs and services for teens give teens who might not be able to visit the library the chance to use the materials and services of the library virtually.

- Using the Internet in order to serve teens provides libraries with opportunities to meet several of the service responses as outlined in PLA's *The New Planning for Results.*

Yes, it might take lots of time and effort to get Internet-based programming and services for teens going in the library. But if they are well planned and successfully integrated into the traditional services of the library, the benefits are sure to be numerous.

NOTES

1. Boston Public Library, Online Tutoring Site, program page. Available at http://www.tutor.com/bpl/about.asp#results. Accessed 10 September 2001.
2. New York Public Library, WordSmiths section of TeenLink, Office of Young Adult Services. Available at http://www2.nypl.org/home/branch/teen/WordSmiths-About.html. Accessed 10 September 2001.
3. Public Library Association, *The New Planning for Results: A Streamlined Approach* (Chicago: ALA, 2001).

4

Making It Happen

As a library creates and designs Internet-based materials and services for young adults, it is important to regularly check that what's being planned will actually work for teens in the community. One of the best ways to do that is to get teens involved in some part of the website-development process. This chapter includes tips for getting teens involved in that process, information on the technology required to successfully publish a website, details on hiring a professional designer or technical specialist, and points to consider when developing a maintenance plan for a library website for teens.

LEARNING BY EXAMPLE

"Every step of the way we went back to the advisory group to show them how far we'd progressed and to get their feedback."[1] That's what Lisa Heggum, teen services librarian at the Pickering Public Library, Ontario, Canada, said when talking about how the library involved teens in the development of their website. At Pickering teens didn't get involved in the nitty-gritty coding of the site, but they did have input into what the site looked like and what content it included. When discussing teen involvement in the development of the website in more detail, Heggum went on to say, "Teens involved in the development of the site have a strong sense of accomplishment, ownership, and pride in the product."[2]

Ownership and pride in product certainly support the developmental assets of empowerment and constructive use of time. Heggum was careful to point out that teen feedback was taken seriously. If the library decided they would not integrate something into the website that the teens suggested, then Heggum explained how and why the decision was made. This helped to make sure the teens involved knew their ideas were taken seriously and they weren't wasting their time by giving their thoughts about the site.

What teens really wanted to include on the site were some interactive features. They thought chat would be great, but since the library doesn't allow chat, Heggum and the library web designer determined that it wouldn't be a good idea to include this as a feature of the site. (The library recently instituted chat reference service so this may eventually have an impact on the teen website.) Heggum explained to the teens involved in putting the site together why chat wasn't going to be included, and they understood. Instead of chat the site provides space for teens to post and read book reviews. Heggum expects to extend this to art and other types of creative work from teens in the near future.

From start to launch the development of the Pickering Public Library teen website, with teen input, took approximately eight months. The process used a lot of back-and-forth communication between the teens involved, Heggum, and the library's web designer. Teens didn't just comment on the content of the site, they also had input on the design. Heggum noted that the first image of a TV the site designer developed was not approved by members of the teen advisory group (TAG). So the designer went back to the "drawing board" and developed something that met with the group's approval (see figure 4-1).

The development of the Pickering teen website was one of the first projects of the library's TAG. Heggum stated that before the group was formed, some in the community didn't understand why it was important to provide teenagers with this type of library pro-

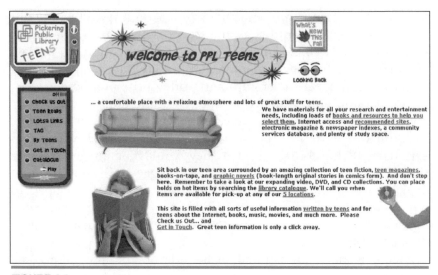

FIGURE 4-1
Pickering Public Library teen website main screen

gram. But because of the success of the teen website, along with other projects in which TAG members were involved, there is a better understanding of the purpose of such a group. As a matter of fact, some of the TAG members attended a library board of trustees meeting to discuss the projects they worked on, including the website. Heggum said, "The website helped the library board understand the importance of services to teens in the community."[3]

HOW TO DO IT—WITH THE HELP OF WEB DESIGNERS OR TECHNICAL SPECIALISTS

As mentioned above, Pickering Public Library involved teens in all of the steps of the development process except for the actual coding of the pages and design of images. (For that they had full-time library staff.) Those wanting to get teens involved in a similar web-development process, the following tips should prove useful:

Find out as much as possible before starting the project about the properties of good websites. Be clear about what makes a website good, and be ready to help teens understand the differences between good and bad web design and why it's important to make sure their site meets basic web-design principles (see figure 4-2).

Choose background and font colors carefully. Colors that might be fun to look at for a couple of minutes (or seconds) could prove to be impossible to look at for long periods of time. If that happens teens won't take advantage of your content.

If using a background image or texture, make sure that it doesn't overpower the content of your site. Teens who visit the site should be able to read what the creators of the site have to say.

Choose the font color and face carefully. Make sure that the color used can be read on the background. Make sure that the face chosen is easy to read.

Choose images carefully. Make sure that they don't take a long time to load and that they don't interfere with the content of your site.

Use images and colors that help create an image for the library's teen services. When teens see the colors and images on the page they should immediately be able to tell where they are.

Provide consistent layout and navigation. Teens will find it a lot easier to move around the site if they can assume what to expect on every page. If on every page teens have to search for navigation or are bombarded with a different design and images, they may turn away and never come back.

Don't make teens burrow down several levels in order to find the information for which they are looking. Storyboard the site in order to get a sense of the navigational flow and to make sure teens can find what they are looking for pretty easily.

Think carefully about how links on every page are labeled. Make sure to use terminology that doesn't just make sense to teens creating the site but will also make sense to teens who visit the site.

Carefully balance the amount of text, images, and blank space on each page. Research shows that it's hard for people to focus when there is too much text on a screen. For that reason it's a good idea not to have pages filled with text that scrolls on and on.

Give people an opportunity to interact with the teens who created the site, either by providing e-mail links for asking questions or FAQ or help pages.

Test the pages on a variety of browsers and browser versions, Lynx, Netscape, Internet Explorer, and AOL. That way all teens who visit the site will see the same thing.

Test the site with a small group of teens, other than those who are helping in the development, before publicizing it to the world.

FIGURE 4-2
Web design tips

Before getting teens involved, make sure to know exactly what aspects of the development process with which they are going to be involved. For example, are teens going to be able to code pages and create images or are they going to spend their time providing ideas and feedback on content and design?

If working with a web designer or technical specialist make sure he understands how teens are going to be involved and will be able to integrate teen feedback into his work. See figures 4-3 and 4-4 for tips on hiring a web designer or technical specialist and questions to ask when interviewing designers and specialists.

Determine a timeline for the design, creation, and launch of the site.

When meeting with teens about the project for the first time, let them know what they will get to do and what the timeline is.

Information about the library. For example, size, services, audience, and so on.

Description of the project and the job available.

Goals of the website—what should it do and accomplish and the audience.

The scope of services the designer or technical specialist should be able to supply. For example, graphic design, coding, logo development, javascript, php, and so on.

Timeline—for the proposal and selection process as well as the website-development process.

Dollars available to the project.

Requirements of proposal to be submitted. For example, description of organization that's applying, information regarding similar projects in which the applying organization has been involved, expertise of those who will be working on the project, how the organization applying envisions what they will create and do for the project, draft timeline, draft budget, references, and where to send the submission.

FIGURE 4-3
What to include in an RFP for a web designer or technical specialist

Spend time with teens talking about the goal of the teen website. Ask for their ideas on how to meet that goal via the website.

Brainstorm with teens ideas of what they would like to see on the website. Let them know that the sky is the limit to start with, but in the long run, the site won't include everything talked about or requested.

Ask teens to consider some of their favorite websites, why the sites are their favorites, and ways the library might integrate similar features into the site they are helping to develop.

Determine the audience for the site. Is it all the teens in the community, just the teens who are helping to develop the site, teens around the world? Ask the teens involved in the project to think about whom the library should serve via the site and then to consider the features that are

---

What are some examples of your previous work? Consider asking designers and technical specialists for examples at different levels of the spectrum. For example, what's an example of a site you have worked on in which the audience didn't have much technical knowledge or access, and what's an example of a site you have worked on for more advanced users?

What web or technical services do you provide? For example, logo design, coding, graphic design, storyboarding, walk-throughs, maintenance, javascript, java, php, cgi, administrative tool development, and so on.

What is your web and technical development process like? For example, what steps would you take in the development of the website? How would you communicate with us? How would you ask for and like to receive feedback?

What is the timeline you would set up for a project like this?

How do you create the page code? For example, do you code by hand or do you use a tool such as Dreamweaver, Front Page, Netscape Composer, and so on?

How do you design for accessibility? For example, what do you include in the code in order to ensure that all users will be able to use and access the site successfully?

FIGURE 4-4
Questions for potential web designers and technical specialists

appropriate to include for the audience selected. As teens consider the audience, make sure they also consider the type of access available to those whom the site will serve.

If working with a web designer or technical specialist, have her meet with the teens to hear what they have to say about the website. Also use this time so the designer or technical specialist can talk to the teens about what she does and how their input will help to improve the site.

Talk with teens involved in the project about ideas for launching and promoting the site.

HOW TO DO IT—WITHOUT THE HELP OF WEB DESIGNERS OR TECHNICAL SPECIALISTS

What if the library doesn't have the advantage of consultants or staff to help with coding, graphic design, and technological features of a site? Then it might be time to involve teens in the process of coding and designing. If that is the case it's still important to cover the topics outlined previously with teens who are involved, but it's also important to help teens learn how to create web pages that meet standards of design and coding that will be acceptable to the community at large. This isn't going to be a teen's personal website where he can use whatever design best shows off his personality. It's the library site and not only needs to support teen needs but also is the library's teen face for the world to see. These tips should prove useful when teens are involved in the coding and design of the site:

Find out about the different skills of the members of the advisory group. For example, are some teens artists, are others writers, do some have a particularly good sense of graphic design? Harness each teen's strengths by assigning her website duties that support those strengths. For example, the artists in the group will create the images, the writers will develop the text, and the graphic designers will create the navigation and layout for the site.

Determine how teens are going to learn coding. Will they need to have coding skills before getting involved in the project or can those skills be learned at the library as a part of the project? Similarly, consider what level of coding skills teens are going to need. Almost anyone can create websites with a little bit of coding knowledge and the help of a coding program; however, that doesn't mean the sites developed will meet the Americans with Disabilities Act (ADA) guidelines or for that matter will work well in all browsers (see figure 4-2). The W3C (World Wide Web Consortium) developed (and now updates) accessibility guidelines. In order to know all the features a website should include to meet ADA requirements it's important to know what's in the W3C documents. More information on the W3C and website-accessibility guidelines is available on the companion website to *Teens.library*. Two of the ADA guidelines important to remember as you create the website are:

- Include the "alt" (alternative) attribute for all images. Each image on the page needs to have text included in the code that describes the image. This provides text that can be read to people who can't see the images because of visual disabilities.

- Make sure all image links have a text equivalent. For example, if images are used for navigation it's important to include text links for each of the navigational components as well. This allows those who can't see the images to have link options that can be read by an electronic text reader.

Be ready to talk to teens about copyright issues as they relate to images on the teen website. It's easy to grab images off the Web to use within a site; however, that doesn't mean it's legal to do so. Find ways to help teens understand the ramifications of using art created by others and the procedures for gaining permission to use someone else's work. This might include brainstorming with teens the reasons it's not legal to use others' work, asking teens to consider how they would feel if someone "stole" writing or art they created and called it their own, and talking about real stories of what has happened to those who have been caught using other people's art on the Web. This could actually open up opportunities to teach some research and information-literacy skills as teens look for information on the ramifications of ignoring copyright laws.

WHAT IT TAKES TO GET ON THE WEB

Chapter 3 discussed the technology required to make specific features as seen on specific teen library websites work. In this section of *Teens.library* an overview of considerations related to the technological features of a site is included. As the library's teen website is developed, it will not be possible to make certain decisions without knowing information about the server on which the website is going to live. For example, if there are plans to integrate forms for feedback or interactive features, it is necessary to know if the server the web pages will live on supports those components. Along with servers it's important to think about the domain name and directory structure that will be used for the site.

One issue that needs to be resolved is the domain name the teen site will use. Will the site simply be within a subdirectory of the main library site, or will it use an entirely different domain name? If the teen site will be in a subdirectory, what will be the name of the main folder in which the teen pages live? For example, if the main address of the library website is http://www.librarysite.org/, and the teen section of the site is called "Teen Central," a subdirectory with the heading "teen central" might be created. The address for the teen site would then be http://www.librarysite.org/teencentral/.

If planning on using a separate domain name for the site, the domain needs to be purchased from a reputable vendor of domain names. There are many resources available for locating and purchasing domain names. For example, a visit to Domain Surfer, http://www.domainsurfer.com/, provides the chance to search for a specific domain name to see if it is taken. If the name is available it can then be registered—for $35 per year—with one of the agencies that provides registration services. (More information on registration services is available on the *Teens.library* companion website.)

It is also important to consider where the teen library pages will live. If using the same domain name as the other pages of the library's website, that question is already answered, as the teen pages will live on the same server as the other pages of the library site. If not within a subdirectory of the library's main site, then it's possible the teen pages might live on another server. In either case, it's important to find out what features the server supports before getting too involved in the development process. The following information complements that provided in chapter 3 to help determine the technology required to support the library's website for teens. (Links to scripts and resources related to each of the following components are available on the *Teens.library* companion website.)

Online Forms

Online forms can be used for feedback, to collect specific information, or as a part of a discussion board. As mentioned in chapter 3 these forms can range from the very simple to the advanced, with the simplest forms requiring nothing more than an e-mail address on the part of the person receiving the form.

Many forms seen on the Web use a script—usually done in Common Gateway Interface (CGI) that interacts with the server in order to parse the information from the form and send it to the receiver successfully. To implement these forms on the teen library website it's important to make sure the server used has a CGI-bin directory. (The person or organization maintaining the server will know if that directory is available.) The CGI-bin directory is where the information that informs the script what it needs to carry out lives. Some companies that provide server space include scripts on their servers that allow for form implementation. In other instances, implementing the form requires creating a script or using one found on another website.

The many resources available for people who can't create or support forms on their website can be useful. These usually free services allow their server space to be used for forms. These sites can prove to be a good place to start in order to create forms that are easy to use; however, as with many free services on the Internet, there are limitations to these types of services. One of these limitations usually is that little or no support is provided to those using the free form service.

Discussion Boards

As discussion boards integrate forms, the choices available in order to implement the technology required are similar to those mentioned previously. At the most basic level a server needs to allow the user to access a CGI-bin directory so that the script used to manage the discussion board can organize messages in an appropriate and orderly fashion. Unlike feedback forms, there is no very low-end solution to implementing this feature. As with feedback forms there are free online services available to help implement the discussion-board feature successfully. There are also websites that provide server space for implementation of discussion boards. (The same caveats, of course, apply.) When considering the best discussion-board option for the purposes of the teen library website, it's important to consider the features provided with the script, software, or online free discussion-board service. Two issues to consider are:

> *Organization of messages.* Are the messages organized in a visual fashion, for example, in folders, so it is easy to see the different discussions and the responses to each discussion?
>
> *Preview capabilities.* Is there a way for those posting messages to preview their posts before submitting and make changes if needed?

Audio or Video

There is a variety of audio or video features that might be included in the teen library website. These include recordings of programs held at the library, interviews with authors, webcasts of library events, and so on. The type of audio or video file created has some impact on how it will be made available on the teen website server.

Audio and video files created in a streaming format (Real Audio and Real Video or Windows Media) can be made available on a "regular" server as long as the appropriate code is used. Special servers are also available to host this type of content, and it is a good idea to check with the server provider to find out if a Real Audio server is available for use by the teen website. Other audio and video files not created in a streaming format can be easily integrated into a web page simply by using the appropriate code. Before deciding what format of audio or video to use it is important to consider the technology available to the site's users. Try to determine the type of access the audience has. Do they have access at a sufficient speed in order to download or stream audio or video in a timely fashion? If not, then these features might simply be beyond the capabilities of the target audience.

Chat

Chat is another feature of the library website that can be implemented in a variety of ways. Software can be used on a local computer or a server in order to make chatting available, and there are also free services that allow visitors to set up chat rooms for limited periods of time. When deciding which type of chat service to implement it's important to think about which will best support the purpose of the chat and the entire teen website.

Software available includes instant messaging programs like Yahoo! Messenger, AOL Instant Messenger, and ICQ. If using one of these programs, information would be provided via the teen library website on the library's instant messaging username so teens could contact young adult library staff or take part in regularly scheduled instant messaging sessions.

There are also software programs that are often used to host reference chat sessions but which can be tweaked in order to fit the needs of a teen chat hosted by the library's young adult services staff. For example, the Cleveland Public Library will be using the 24/7 Reference product in order to hold chat sessions between teens and young adult authors. The product was not designed for this purpose, but it certainly can be used this way. To use a software program of this type, the library needs to purchase or contract to use the software and install it on a server. Once the software is available the library then needs to work with the vendor to make any changes necessary to create an interface that will work for an author chat as well as a reference chat.

There are many other pieces of software available that libraries can install onto a server to provide chatting capabilities. When considering which software to select, some issues to consider are:

How many people can chat at the same time?

What features are available to chatters? For example, can they use different colors for their messages? Are icons or sounds available for helping chatters describe their thoughts and feelings?

Are there any video and audio capabilities for the chat?

Is it possible to hide certain chatters or communicate with a specified chatter in private?

One other chat option is to set up chat rooms with a service like Yahoo! Chat. User-created chat rooms at Yahoo! are only available for the time in which there are chatters in the room. Also, in order to access the chat room, each chatter needs a user-name and password, which means before accessing the chat a registration form needs to be filled out. When using Yahoo! Chat, a wide variety of features will be available to the chatters—colored text, icons and audio, and so on—but because of the registration some teens might not be able to take part.

Previous chapters of *Teens.library* explored a wide array of ideas for the types of content and interactivity a library might integrate into its website for teens. Before making any final decisions about those features it's important to consider the tools available for creating and hosting these services and determine which will work best for the library and for the teens in the community.

EVALUATION, STATISTICS, AND USER TESTING

Don't forget the need to gather statistics about the use of the teen library website. It's possible the server used by the library or the server selected to host the teen site provides statistical information about site use. If not, there are software packages available for purchase that provide the type of information needed. Included in many of these packages are statistics about where visitors to the site came from (what website they were visiting before visiting the library's site), the searches visitors did in order to find the site, the browsers visitors most often use, the validity of the links within the site, and so on. A selection of links to statistics software is available on the *Teens.library* companion website.

Don't begin evaluation of the website after the launch has occurred. It's important to make sure that teens in the community, other than those who worked on the development of the site, have an opportunity to provide their ideas about the site before launch. This can be done through focus groups or special web-evaluation sessions with teens in the community. The feedback gathered in these sessions can prove to be very useful.

Teens who don't ever come into the library are an audience you want to seek out to get their feedback on the site. Contact local schools, youth groups, religious institutions, and so on, to locate teen testers. It's possible to hold focus groups online so that teens will not have to come to the library to participate. This can be done by providing the URL to the group of testers and asking them to look over the site. Then host an e-mail chat or discussion-board discussion with the teens in order to get their feedback.

If hosting a live focus group to get teen feedback make sure it's possible for each teen participant to have a computer to view the site on his own. During the focus group provide teens with time to go through the site. Then bring the group together and give them a chance to discuss what they liked and didn't like about it.

Another option is to do one-on-one testing with teens. In this instance, someone—a library staff member or teen who helped in the development of the site—would sit with a teen tester. The tester would click through the site looking at the different components. The person sitting with the teen would pay attention to the navigation choices and comments made during the "click-through" and then would ask questions of the tester based on what she saw.

Before any user-testing discussion starts, prepare questions that will provide you with the information needed to know how well the site works with those outside of the development group. Work with the teens who helped develop the site to create questions that will provide meaningful information about the site (see figure 4-5 for sample questions).

1. What's the first thing that came to your mind when you saw the website?

2. What's the first thing that you looked at when you got to the site?

3. If you could add one thing to the site what would it be, and why?

4. What one thing would you delete from the site, and why?

5. What word would you use to describe the colors used on the site?

6. What word would you use to describe the images on the site?

7. Did you have any trouble figuring out how to get to different parts of the site? What's an example of that?

8. Have you seen other sites that have similar kinds of information? If you have, can you remember what they are? Did you like this site more or less, and why?

9. Would you visit this site again? Why or why not?

10. What would you like the people who created the site to know about how you would or would not use it?

FIGURE 4-5
Sample user-testing questions

No matter what type of testing is done it is key to pay attention to what teens didn't understand about the site, when clicks led to unexpected resources, and so on. Look for instances when navigation, content, or labels have to be explained to focus group participants. Those are opportunities to revise and create something that doesn't need explanation before successful use. Remember, many of the teens who use the site won't have training before doing so. Most likely they will access the site from a remote location. That means they need to be able to figure out how it works all on their own. If it's too hard to figure it out then they won't stay at or return to the site.

Similarly, no matter what method is used for the user testing it's important to make sure that whoever is involved in facilitating the testing is able to proceed with an open mind. Those leading the discussions or working with testers one-on-one should not react to the comments made in a positive or negative way. Teens involved in the testing of the site will need to have training in order to work with their peers in this manner. Teens should have a strong sense of the purpose of the testing, why it's important to test the site with teens other than those involved in the development, how to react unemotionally to feedback, and how to take information provided and use it to improve and enhance the site.

In most instances, it is important to test throughout the development process. If a teen advisory group is involved in the development it's possible that less outside testing is required. However, if not working directly with teens in the development of the site, it's important to host a few testing sessions throughout the process. By doing that it will be less likely that there will be surprises about what teens think of and how they use the site when it is close to completion. Make sure to avoid having to make major changes once the design and navigation are fully developed.

SITE MAINTENANCE

Links are just one of the aspects of the site that need maintenance once it is up and running. If not using link-checking software, someone will need to check the links frequently to make sure they are still valid. Other maintenance issues that certainly come into play include:

- If the site includes information about library programs, it is essential to keep that information current, taking down old information and replacing it with new information.
- If the site includes information about materials recently added to the library collection, it's important to keep that list of materials current so that teens visiting the site will be able to tell what the newest items in the library are.
- If the site includes book reviews, comments, and so on, by teens, it's important to determine the best way to archive old entries and make way for the new. Scrolling through several dozen, or perhaps hundreds, of entries isn't fun for anyone.

In other words, once the site is launched, only part of the work is done. Updating and maintaining the pages is a time-consuming but important part of the process. Teens of course can be involved in this process, particularly if they have coding and design skills. Or if not purchasing a piece of software to check links on the site, consider asking teens to check links on a regular basis. Part of their job could be to fill out an online form to report dead links. Other ways teens can help in the maintenance process include:

> Reading, viewing, and weeding submissions to various writing and art pages on the site. Teens who help develop the site can also develop a set of criteria for the posting of work by their peers. They then can use the criteria developed to evaluate the materials submitted to the site.

> Developing discussion topics for chat or discussion-board features on the site. For example, teens in the community might select the topic for discussion and develop the initial posting for a discussion thread or moderate and facilitate a chat on the particular topic. They might also select appropriate print and web-based materials that support the topic that would then be noted on a website that complements the event.

> Setting up archiving procedures for materials added to the site. Teens working on the development of the website would develop a schedule for archiving stories, poems, reviews, and so on, posted on the website. They would then review the materials on the site and determine which are ready for archiving.

Make sure that the teens helping in the website-development process realize their job is not done when the site goes live. As the site gets used, teens and librarians will discover a variety of changes they want to make to improve and enhance what they started with. Simple changes and enhancements will be part of the ongoing maintenance process. But, of course, a time will come when a redesign is in order. Then it's time to get ready to start the process again!

NOTES

1. Lisa Heggum, phone conversation with Linda W. Braun, September 18, 2001.
2. Ibid.
3. Ibid.

APPENDIX

A

Teen Website Development Checklist

The name of the site is: _____

The site will live on this server: _____

The address of the site will be: _____

The project timeline is: _____

GOALS AND AUDIENCE

The website goals are: _____

_____

_____

The primary teen audience the site will serve is:

☐ 12 to 18 year olds   ☐ 12 to 14 year olds

☐ 15 to 18 year olds   ☐ Other _____

The majority of the audience will access the site

☐ Through a dial-up   ☐ High-speed connection
    connection   (DSL or cable)

☐ At school   ☐ At a friend's   ☐ At home

☐ Other _____

65

CONTENT

Included on the website will be:

☐ Links   ☐ Feedback forms   ☐ Electronic pathfinders

☐ Discussion boards   ☐ Chat

☐ Book reviews   ☐ Readers' advisory tools   ☐ Audio or video

☐ Other _____

_____

☐ The content for these sections is under development   ☐ The content for these sections is complete

DESIGN AND NAVIGATION

The labels we'll use for the main sections of the site are:

1.   3.   5.

2.   4.   6.

☐ The navigation and information architecture of the site is under development

☐ The navigation and information architecture of the site is completed

☐ A flow chart or storyboard has been developed for the site

The color scheme of the site is: _____

IMAGES

☐ The logo for the site is developed

☐ The images for the site are being created or gathered

☐ All of the images for the site have been created or gathered

TECHNOLOGICAL REQUIREMENTS

☐ cgi-bin access is available on the server   ☐ Chat software has been installed

☐ Discussion forum scripts created   ☐ Real audio or video server is available

☐ Feedback form scripts created   ☐ Free feedback or survey form servers evaluated and selected

☐ Free discussion-forum servers evaluated and selected   ☐ Other

SITE TESTING

☐ Tested for browser, platform, and ADA compatibility

☐ Revised based on compatibility testing

USER TESTING

☐ Live focus groups scheduled

☐ Online focus groups scheduled

☐ One-on-one "click-throughs" scheduled

☐ User-testing questions are prepared

☐ User testing completed

☐ Other _____

LAUNCH

☐ Scheduled   ☐ Advertised   ☐ Held

Checklist for Teen Involvement in Website Development

Teens will be involved in the following aspects of the web-development process:_____

_____

- ☐ Web designer, technical specialists, and staff working on the project know the role teens will play in the development process
- ☐ Meetings scheduled
- ☐ Advertising about the project distributed
- ☐ Teens registered or selected for the program
- ☐ Role in the development process explained to teens
- ☐ Project timeline discussed
- ☐ Skills of teens who will be involved in coding and graphic design assessed

Teens taking part in coding and graphic design assigned specific tasks
- ☐ HTML
- ☐ Writing
- ☐ Navigation and information architecture
- ☐ Image development
- ☐ Other

☐ Brainstorming and selection of website goals completed

☐ Audience and most common forms of access determined

☐ Brainstorming of possible features and content of the site completed

☐ Brainstorming on principles of web design and what makes a good and bad site for teens done

☐ Technological capabilities of the site server and technical specialists (who might be the teens themselves) determined

☐ Features and content of the site selected

☐ Information architecture developed

☐ Labels of site links selected

☐ Content developed

☐ Images created or gathered

☐ Discussion of copyright

☐ Coding completed

☐ Site tested for browser, platform, and ADA compatibility

☐ Site revised based on results of compatibility testing

☐ Teens take part in user-testing training

☐ User testing scheduled

☐ User testing completed

☐ Site revised based on user-testing findings

☐ Brainstorming on launch advertising and programming

☐ Advertising and programming for launch selected

☐ Launch scheduled

☐ Launch advertising created and distributed

☐ Launch programming planned

☐ Launch

C

Programming Opportunities for Teens Involved in the Development of the Library's Website

HOW'D THEY DO THAT?
Basics of Web-Page Creation and Design

Host a workshop series for teens on creating websites. This should be hands-on where teens learn the code required to make web pages, find out about copyright as it relates to web design, evaluate websites to determine qualities of good web design, and learn problem solving and troubleshooting skills as they write and debug code. The series should be a minimum of four weeks and, if possible, twice that amount of time.

IS IT ANY GOOD?

Sponsor an online program in which teens submit evaluation forms of websites as a means of coming up with a set of design, content, and navigation criteria to use in the development of the library website. This requires the creation of a feedback form that is posted on the library website. Teens would develop a list of sites they would like to evaluate in order to develop their own set of criteria. Links to the sites would be available online, and each time a teen looks at one of the sites she would fill out the form. After the process is completed teens would collate the data, consider the information collected, and then use that information to develop a set of evaluation criteria for their own use.

WEB DESIGNER CHAT

Contact the designer of a website that teens enjoy visiting and ask him to participate in a real-time chat with the teens involved in the creation of the site. During the chat teens could hear what the life of a designer is like and ask questions about their own ideas for the library site. A simple way to implement this chat would be to use ICQ, AIM, or Yahoo! Messenger.

D

Teen Website Evaluation Checklist

Site Name:_____

Site URL: _____

Site Author: _____

Site Sponsor: _____

The best thing about this site is:_____

_____

_____

The worst thing about this site is:_____

_____

_____

I have this to say about the colors used on the site:_____

_____

_____

I have this to say about the images used on the site:_____

_____

_____

I think the information on the site is:

☐ Current   ☐ Out of date   ☐ True   ☐ False

The people behind the site:

☐ Are qualified to write   ☐ Are not qualified to write about
    about this topic   this topic

The reason someone created this site is to:

☐ Teach something   ☐ Entertain

☐ Sell something   ☐ Other _____

☐ It's not easy for me to find   ☐ It's easy for me to find my way
    my way around site and   around site and locate what
    locate what I'm looking for   I'm looking for

Thinking about what I wrote above, this is what I'd tell a friend about the
site:_____

_____

_____

User-Testing Tips

1. Let the teens know what they are there for and what they are expected to help you with.

2. Set a tone so that everyone involved feels that all comments are welcome and will be taken seriously.

3. After you ask a question sit back and give teens the chance to answer. In other words, be quiet.

4. Feel free to ask teens to explain what they said more fully.

5. In the notes that you take include what teens talk about as well as your own thoughts about the responses to the questions.

6. As soon as possible after the testing go over the notes from the session with the teens and highlight the most important points.

SOURCE: Adapted from a handout, "Interviews and Focus Group Tips and Techniques," developed by Alan Brickman, November 1999.

URL INDEX

A

All Game Guide
http://www.allgame.com/

Alloy
http://www.alloy.com/

AOL Instant Messenger
http://www.aol.com/aim/
homenew.adp/

Ask Jeeves
http://www.aj.com/

B

Beliefnet
http://129.33.230.60/

Bolt
http://www.bolt.com/

Boston Public Library Online
Tutoring
http://www.tutor.com/bpl/
Default.asp/

C

Chapter-a-Day
http://www.chapteraday.com/

Cleveland Public Library,
Homework Now
http://www.homeworknow.net/

Cold Fusion
http://www.macromedia.com/
software/coldfusion/

Consumer Education for Teens
http://www.wa.gov/ago/youth/

Curtis Memorial Library, Teen
Zone, Book a Librarian
http://www.curtislibrary.com/
teenzone/booklibrarian.html/

D

Domain Surfer
http://www.domainsurfer.com/

DoSomething
http://www.dosomething.org/

SUBJECT INDEX

Linda W. Braun is an educational technology consultant and an adjunct faculty member at the Lesley University Technology in Education graduate program and the University of Maine (Augusta) Library and Information Technology Distance Education program. Her background is in children's and young adult librarianship, and she is the web manager for YALSA. Her publications include articles in *School Library Journal, NetConnect,* and the *New England Library Association Newsletter* as well as two books published by Neal-Schuman in 2001: *The Internet for Young Learners* and *The Browsable Classroom.* Braun has developed a companion website for this book where you can find more information on the topics covered as well as links to all the URLs mentioned. It is at http://www.leonline.com/Teens.library.